REAL-LIFE GHOST STORIES

SPINE-TINGLING TRUE TALES

AUBRE ANDRUS, MEGAN COOLEY PETERSON, AND EBONY JOY WILKINS

CAPSTONE PRESS
a capstone imprint

Real-Life Ghost Stories is published by Capstone Press,
an imprint of Capstone.
1710 Roe Crest Drive, North Mankato, Minnesota 56003
www.capstonepub.com

Library of Congress Cataloging-in-Publication Data is available on the Library of Congress website.

ISBN: 978-1-4966-8611-4 (paperback)

Image Credits
Alamy: AF archive, 69, age fotostock, 102, Chris Hellier, 31, Chronicle, 25, Collection Christophel © 2013
Warner Bros Entertainment, 89, 91, 93, De Luan, 42, PRISMA ARCHIVO, 41, TCD/Prod.DB, 71, Trinity Mirror/
Mirrorpix, 109; Bridgeman Images: Museo Nacional de Antropologia, Mexico City, Mexico/De Agostini
Picture Library/Archivio J. Lange, 13, Private Collection/PVDE, 49; Courtesy of Tennessee State Library and
Archives: 100, 111, 118; Getty Images: Bettmann, 86–87, Kaz Chiba, 61, Russell McPhedran/Fairfax Media, 85;
iStockphoto: Bassador, 17, sdominick, 83, urbazon, 11; Newscom: akg-images, 33, Alberto E. Tamargo/Sipa
USA, 90, Doug Meszler/Splash News, 27; Shutterstock: ADragan, 117, Africa Studio, 112, Aleshyn_Andrei,
38, andreiuc88, 23, Anna Kogut, 58, Anne Greenwood, 53, avtk, design element, Bob Orsillo, 105, Chantal
de Bruijne, design element, ChiccoDodiFC, 54, Chinnapong, 57 (ribbon), Dale A Stork, 46, daniilphotos, 74,
Dmitry Laudin, cover, Dragana Djorovic, 45, dzentry, 79, Everett Historical, 115, Fer Gregory, 14, 73 (bottom
left), Giraphics, design element, GoMixer, design element, Hitdelight, 103 (top), Igor Sokolov, 57 (scissors),
igorstevanovic, 57 (bible), InnaPoka, 101, Joe Therasakdhi, 81, Lario Tus, 19, 20, 29, LiskaM, 107, Lusica, 113,
MagicDogWorkshop, design element, NikhomTreeVector, design element, NinaMalyna, design element
(black frame), Olivier Le Queinec, 77, Peter Horrox, 72, PeterVrabel, 50–51, Prokrida, design element (gold
frame), design element (silver frame), Stefan Rotter, 106, Tom Tom, 9, Yupa Watchanakit, 15; Wikimedia:
Brian Stansberry, 99, 121, Www78, 123

Editorial Credits
Editor: Eliza Leahy; Designer: Brann Garvey; Media Researcher: Tracy Cummins;
Production Specialist: Kathy McColley

Direct Quotations
Pages 17–18, 22: Radford, Benjamin. *Mysterious New Mexico: Miracles, Magic, and Monsters in the Land of
Enchantment.* Albuquerque: University of New Mexico Press, 2014, 225–226, 234–235.
Page 70: http://www.theoccultmuseum.com/the-conjuring-the-true-story-of-the-perron-family-haunting/
Pages 80–81, 84: https://www.providencejournal.com/breaking-news/content/20130718-film-the-conjuring-
depicts-familys-reported-experience-with-paranormal-activity-in-burrillville-farmhouse-in-70s.ece
Page 90: https://www.ranker.com/list/true-story-behind-the-conjuring-movie/jacob-shelton
Page 90: https://www.trespassmag.com/qa-andrea-and-cynthia-perron-subjects-of-the-conjuring/
Pages 108, 114, 116: Ingram, M.V. *An Authenticated History of the Famous Bell Witch.* Clarksville, TN: W. P. Titus,
printer, 1894, 53, 57–58, 91.

Printed and bound in China.
002730

TABLE OF CONTENTS

LA LLORONA

THE LEGENDARY WEEPING WOMAN OF MEXICO

—◆◇◈ BY MEGAN COOLEY PETERSON ◈◇◆—

TABLE OF CONTENTS

BEWARE THE WEEPING WOMAN

It's late at night, and you're roasting marshmallows with your family at a campsite beside a river. The flames crackle. Moonlight glints off the rushing water. Suddenly you hear a woman cry out for her lost children. But you don't see anyone. As you explore the riverbank, a woman in white drifts toward you. Her feet don't touch the ground. You scream, and she vanishes. Were your eyes playing tricks on you? Or did you just encounter La Llorona, the weeping woman of Mexico?

FACT

La Llorona means "weeping woman" in Spanish.

The story of La Llorona began sweeping through Mexico in the 1500s. According to the tale, a local woman drowned her children. Filled with regret and overtaken by heartache, the woman searched for her children up and down the river. She didn't stop her search even to eat or drink, and she died. Her spirit was doomed to roam the earth forever, calling out for her lost children.

La Llorona's story is still told today. Many people say the weeping woman is not a legend at all but a real ghost. **Skeptics** say that sightings of La Llorona can be explained by mist or lights. They believe there is no ghostly woman in white. Turn the page and decide for yourself.

CHAPTER ONE

THE LEGEND OF LA LLORONA

The legend of La Llorona has terrified listeners for hundreds of years. There is no single story of La Llorona. The most common version involves a beautiful peasant woman. When her husband dies, the woman must raise their children alone. She meets a wealthy man and falls in love. But the man doesn't want to help raise her children. He won't marry her.

Desperate to be with the man she loves, the woman takes her children to the river and drowns them. But after killing them, she dies from a broken heart.

FACT

The story of La Llorona is sometimes told to keep children from misbehaving. Parents warn their children that if they're not careful, La Llorona will get them.

The woman's story doesn't end with her death. Her spirit roams rivers and other bodies of water as she searches for her dead children. Dressed all in white, she cries out for them. Any children who are careless near water are snatched away by La Llorona's tormented ghost.

SKEPTIC'S NOTE

No child abductions have ever been tied to La Llorona or a ghost. If they happened as frequently as reported, there would be **evidence**.

TALES FROM MEXICO

Other versions of La Llorona's legend have spread throughout Mexico. In one story, a poor woman is left by the man she loves. She becomes depressed. While her sons sleep, she kills them. Then she takes her own life. Her ghost wanders the city streets at night, crying out, "*¡Mis hijos!* My sons!"

In another version, a mother drowns her children in a canal. No one knows why she kills her children. Her ghost wears all white and roams the city streets at night. She cries out for her dead children before disappearing into the darkness.

La Llorona is also said to haunt Mexico's highlands. At dusk, she appears to men returning from working in the fields. She calls to them in the voices of their wives or girlfriends. La Llorona leads the men to the edges of cliffs. Any man who follows her ghostly cries is pushed off the cliff to his death.

FACT

In **folklore**, a **siren** was a beautiful creature. She was half-bird, half-human. Sirens used their voices to lure sailors to their deaths.

CIHUACOATL

Some scholars say La Llorona is based on the **Aztec** goddess Cihuacoatl. The Aztecs lived in present-day Mexico long before the Spanish arrived. According to legend, Cihuacoatl stole infants and killed them. Dressed in white, she drifted along the streets after she killed them, wailing. Her cries warned of wars and misery.

LA LLORONA HAUNTS THE UNITED STATES

Mexican immigrants brought the tale of La Llorona with them to the southwestern United States. Like in Mexico, there are many U.S. versions of her story. Some say her children can be seen wandering the streets at night. Other tales say that La Llorona isn't a ghost at all—she's alive and bloodthirsty.

In another twist on the legend, La Llorona doesn't kill her children. On a cold night, she decides to leave her husband. She hides her children under a bridge on the shore of a river. Then she goes home to pack their belongings. But when she returns, the children have frozen to death. She haunts the river, weeping for her children.

FACT

In New Mexico, La Llorona's soul is sometimes associated with flames or balls of fire.

FOLKTALES AND URBAN LEGENDS

Folktales have been told for thousands of years. They are stories or legends passed from person to person. Urban legends are modern versions of folktales shared by word of mouth and online. Urban legends can be strange or scary— or both. They often deal with real-life fears, such as drowning or talking to strangers. Urban legends sometimes contain a lesson by telling us what *not* to do.

CHAPTER TWO

ENCOUNTERS WITH LA LLORONA

Is La Llorona a legend or a real ghost? Some people claim to have come face-to-face with the weeping woman. These real-life encounters will send chills up your spine. But are they enough to convince you she's more than just a scary story?

WALKING ON WATER

In 1931, a girl named Guadalupe visited the Santa Fe River in New Mexico with her two brothers. The boys spent the summer afternoon splashing in the cool water. Guadalupe played on the riverbank. Suddenly, a gust of wind tore through the river valley. It rattled the weeds and cattails where Guadalupe played. Then she heard the sound of tinkling bells.

SKEPTIC'S NOTE

Some skeptics say people mistake fog or shadows for La Llorona. People who "hear" the ghost are actually hearing howling animals or blowing wind.

Guadalupe tried to move, but she found herself paralyzed. "I could not move a muscle," she later recalled. "I was mesmerized by the sound of the bells for at least a minute." Once the sound of the bells died away, Guadalupe heard a woman crying: "*Mija, mija*. My daughter, my daughter." Finally able to move, Guadalupe and her brothers ran all the way home. Guadalupe's brothers also heard the woman calling out. But they heard her crying for her sons, not her daughter.

Guadalupe and her brothers recounted their tale to their parents. Guadalupe's mother whispered to her father, "La Llorona!" The family quickly returned to the river to see if they could find her. The woman could still be heard wailing. Guadalupe's mother shouted, "Leave my children alone, daughter of the devil!"

As the family turned to leave, one of Guadalupe's brothers yelled for them to stop. He pointed to the river. A ghostly figure walked on the water, her arms outstretched. The family fled in terror.

FROZEN WITH FEAR

Between 2000 and 2009, a young boy was visiting family in Durango, Mexico. He played outside with his cousins late at night. Suddenly, the boy found himself separated from his family. The hairs on the back of his neck stood up straight. The boy could feel something—or someone—watching him. When the boy heard the laughter of unfamiliar children, he became paralyzed with fear.

SKEPTIC'S NOTE

When faced with danger, people experience a fight-or-flight response. Scientists say that people often freeze while deciding whether to fight or run away.

Soon the laughter died out, and a woman began to wail. She begged for her children to return to her. Fearing it was La Llorona, the boy was finally able to move. He ran into his grandmother's house. Everyone inside the house had also heard the woman's cries. Was it La Llorona? Or is there another explanation?

FACT

In Santa Fe, New Mexico, La Llorona is said to haunt the Public Employees Retirement Association building near the Santa Fe River. Employees have heard wailing in the halls. Others report being pushed by unseen hands.

THE GHOST WITHOUT EYES

Two brothers in Texas got the fright of a lifetime near the city of Peñitas in the mid-2010s. They were driving home in separate cars on Military Road around midnight. This barren road runs along the Rio Grande River. As darkness settled, the brothers noticed a woman walking along the side of the road. She wore a long, white dress and no shoes. And she was soaking wet.

Concerned for her safety, the brother in the front car slowed down to ask her if she needed a ride home. The pale woman slowly turned toward the car. Her face was unlike any he had ever seen. She had gaping black holes where her eyes should be. The man sped away in his car. When he glanced in the rearview mirror, she was gone. His brother in the rear car also could not see her once he passed.

SKEPTIC'S NOTE

If the man pulled up next to the woman, his car's headlights would not have been pointing at her. Her eyes may have been simply hidden in shadow.

WHAT'S YOUR NAME?

Around this same time in Santa Maria, Texas, a young girl rode her bike to her cousin's house late at night. Her cousin lived near a cemetery close to the Rio Grande River. Just as she parked her bike in the driveway, a woman in white appeared. She hovered above the ground. Then the woman floated toward the girl, who was frozen in shock. Finally the woman asked, "Who are you?" The girl managed to answer with a fake name before running into the house. When she looked back, the mysterious woman had vanished. Had the girl spoken to La Llorona?

FACT

In some tales, La Llorona is 9 feet (2.7 meters) tall. In others, her face is a bare skull.

THE GHOSTLY HITCHHIKER

A winter's drive home turned into a nightmare for one man from Pecos, New Mexico. He was driving home late one night in 1953. His car's headlights lit up a woman standing alone on the side of the road. She wore a long, black cloak that covered most of her face. The man pulled over and opened the passenger's door. "Would you like a ride home?" he asked. The woman climbed into the car without answering.

As the man drove, the woman sat still as a statue. She kept one hand on her knee and the other inside her cloak. The man still couldn't make out her face. He tried to ask her questions, but she refused to utter a single word. Soon, the man began to smell sulfur. Nervous, he pulled the car over to ask her to get out. But when he turned toward his silent passenger, she was gone. The woman had never even opened the door to get out. Before the man could drive away, a bloodcurdling scream pierced the car's interior. The hairs on his neck stood straight up.

The man later told his friend what he had experienced. His friend had a shocking story of his own—he had also encountered the mysterious woman. "That was La Llorona!" said the man's friend. Even though the ghostly hitchhiker wore all black, the men believed the woman could be none other than La Llorona.

THE VANISHING HITCHHIKER

The Vanishing Hitchhiker is one of the best-known urban legends. It is told all over the world. In most versions, a driver sees a person on the side of the road. The driver offers them a ride. While driving, the driver notices the hitchhiker has vanished. The driver learns later that this person had already died. Sometimes the hitchhiker leaves something behind, like a jacket or footprint.

23

CHAPTER THREE

LADIES IN WHITE AROUND THE WORLD

La Llorona isn't the only ghostly woman in white. "White lady" ghost stories have been told around the world for hundreds of years. People use these stories to help them deal with and understand death.

BANSHEES

The banshee is a female spirit from Irish folklore. According to legend, banshees can be heard wailing at night. In Ireland, they are considered messengers of death. If a person hears a banshee's cries, someone in their family is doomed to die.

Like La Llorona, banshees are often said to wear all white. They are typically described as old women with long, white hair. They have red-rimmed eyes from crying so much.

FACT

Like La Llorona, banshees are often associated with bodies of water. In Irish **mythology**, water is a gateway to the underworld.

Banshees are common in Scottish folklore. In Scotland, a banshee-like being is known as *bean-nighe*. They are said to be found near rivers.

FACT

The White Lady is one of the Philippines' most famous ghosts. Sightings of her are often reported on Balete Drive in Manila. She is said to haunt cab drivers.

HAUNTED FRANCE

Ghostly women in white are also said to haunt France. Some haunt bridges, ravines, roads, and creeks. Travelers who want to pass must show respect to the ghost. According to some legends, the ghost extends her hand, asking for a dance. She lets travelers pass if they dance with her. But if the traveler refuses, the lady in white flings them into a ditch filled with thorns. Some ladies in white have **familiars**, or animals under their control. If a traveler doesn't show respect, the ghost commands her familiars to attack them.

FACT

In France, the white lady ghost is sometimes called *La Dame Blanche*.

WHITE LADY AT THE LAKE

In Rochester, New York, a ghostly figure dressed in white haunts Durand Eastman Park. According to legend, a mother and daughter lived in the area in the early 1800s. One night, the daughter went for a walk on the beach of Lake Ontario. She never returned.

Her mother searched the beach and surrounding woods for the rest of her life. Even after the mother died, her spirit never gave up her search. On misty nights, a ghostly woman in white has been spotted floating over the waves.

A storm ripped through Durand Eastman Park, and a strange figure emerged in the bark of a tree that had been damaged by wind. Some people believe this figure to be the ghost of the White Lady. •

GERMANY'S LADIES IN WHITE

One of the earliest-known lady in white stories came from Germany in the mid-1400s. German white lady ghosts are called *die weisse Frau*. *Die weisse Frau* means "the white lady" in German. Some scholars believe this story was carried to Mexico by Spanish explorers. It may have inspired the tale of La Llorona.

According to the German story, a rich man died. He left behind a widow and two children. His widow hoped to remarry and soon drew the attention of a wealthy man. But the man said he would not marry her because "four eyes" were in the way. The widow assumed he meant the "four eyes" of her children. While her children slept one night, she crept into their bedroom and killed them.

When the man found out the widow had murdered her children, he rejected her. The "four eyes" he had referred to were those of his parents. They did not approve of the widow. The widow later opened a **convent** and became a nun. After her death, she haunted the convent. Her ghostly **apparition** signaled death to anyone unlucky enough to see her.

A MURDEROUS GHOST

In another German white lady tale, a young peasant girl
meets a rich man. They have a baby together, but the man
won't marry her. In a rage, the woman kills the man and
their child. She is arrested and locked away, and after a
short time she goes insane and dies. Her ghost wears
a long, white gown. Anyone who speaks to this
white lady dies within a few days.

CHAPTER FOUR

WAS LA LLORONA A REAL PERSON?

The tale of La Llorona has been told for hundreds of years in Mexico and the southwestern United States. Her story warns children to be safe around water. It also teaches parents to look after their children. But could La Llorona have been a real woman?

Some believe La Llorona may be the ghost of a native Mexican woman named La Malinche. In the early 1500s, Spanish explorer Hernán Cortés sailed to Mexico. He wanted to take the land from the Aztecs. Cortés took La Malinche as a slave. La Malinche spoke both Spanish and the Aztec language of Nahuatl. She helped Cortés speak with Aztec leaders. She also had a son with him.

FACT

The film *The Curse of La Llorona* debuted in 2019. Cast members said they felt a ghostly presence on set.

Cortés took the Aztecs' land by force in 1521, ending the Aztec Empire. Some stories say that La Malinche felt guilty for helping Cortés. They say she spent her remaining days weeping over her betrayal of the Aztecs. Her weeping has been connected to the tale of La Llorona.

SKEPTIC'S NOTE

In reality, La Malinche married a Spanish man and had more children. No historical records support the idea that she spent her life in misery.

La Malinche was born with the name Malinal and has also been known as Malintzin and Doña Marina.

THE WEEPING WOMAN OF MEXICO

Tales of ghostly women in white aren't limited to Mexico and the southwestern United States. Different versions of these tales have been told around the world in many different cultures. Though the stories differ, they share many common threads. These ghosts often wear white but not always. They cry out to warn others of death or danger. People often tell these stories as a way to make sense of an uncertain world.

Most writers and scholars agree that La Llorona is an urban legend. Her story is used as a cautionary tale. Like most urban legends, it has many variations. In some, La Llorona weeps for the children she killed. In others, she is a beautiful woman who lures men to their deaths. No matter the story, the name La Llorona instills fear into everyone who hears it. So listen carefully the next time the sun goes down. You just might hear the weeping woman of Mexico.

MEDEA

The story of Medea from Greek mythology has a lot of similarities to the tale of La Llorona. Medea was a witch who was able to predict the future. She used her powers to help her husband, Jason, steal a sacred object from her father. Jason later left Medea for another woman. Like La Llorona, Medea killed her children. But she showed no **remorse** for their deaths.

According to legend, after killing her children, Medea later married Aegeus. She eventually attempted to poison his son, Theseus.

BLOODY MARY

GHOST OF A QUEEN?

BY AUBRE ANDRUS

TABLE OF CONTENTS

THE LEGEND OF BLOODY MARY

The bathroom is dark, and the door is closed. The only noise is your breath, slow and steady. A flickering candle casts a soft glow on your face. You stare into the mirror and begin whispering, "Bloody Mary, Bloody Mary, Bloody Mary . . ."

This **ritual** has been a popular—and scary!—slumber party game in the United States since the 1970s. It's a fear test that only the brave dare play. Why? Because if you believe the legend, chanting "Bloody Mary" in front of a mirror will **summon** an angry spirit.

Those who've played this game claim to see the reflection of a woman. But what she looks like and what happens next is up for debate. Some say she's an evil witch. Others claim to see a gruesome corpse. Some viewers see red tears drip down her face, or a dead baby in her arms. She may scream, curse, or even reach out of the mirror to scratch your face bloody with her long fingernails.

Skeptics think that sightings of Bloody Mary could be explained by people's eyes playing tricks on them. But legend says this terrifying spirit steals the souls of those who call upon her. Anyone who plays the game could be strangled, trapped in the mirror, or haunted by Bloody Mary's ghost forever.

MYSTERY OF MIRRORS

The ancient Romans believed a person's reflection was their soul. Breaking a mirror meant your soul would be damaged for seven years. They weren't the only ones who believed this. Some cultures believe that covering mirrors with a sheet after someone dies can help the deceased person's soul move on to the **afterworld**. Other cultures believe in covering mirrors every night before they go to sleep. And some believe they shouldn't look in a mirror at night for fear they will get sick or die.

CHAPTER ONE

BLOODY MARY IN REAL LIFE

Nobody knows for sure who Bloody Mary was or why she **allegedly** appears in the reflections of mirrors around the world. There are many different people whom the legend of Bloody Mary could be based on, including English royalty, an accused witch, and an evil murderer. Depending on which version you believe, there are different ways to summon her and different reasons she appears.

SKEPTIC'S NOTE

People disagree as to how many times Bloody Mary should be repeated—anywhere from three to one hundred times. And others disagree on exactly what to say. Some versions of the tale repeat longer phrases, such as, "Bloody Mary, I have your baby." Still others perform various actions such as flushing the toilet, blowing out a candle, or spinning around three times.

Mary Tudor ruled England from 1553–1558. Her reign was marked by her **persecution** of Protestants.

QUEEN MARY I

Are you brave enough to chant the phrases "Bloody Mary, I stole your baby" or "Bloody Mary, I killed your baby"? The image that appears in the mirror is often said to be the ghost of Queen Mary I. Legend says that she is unhappily searching for a missing child.

Thomas Cranmer was a leader of the Protestants.
He was burned alive during Queen Mary I's reign.

Mary Tudor became the first queen of England in 1553. Although she only ruled for five years, she was a queen no one could forget. She believed that everyone should follow her religion, Roman Catholicism. Those who didn't were burned alive. They were known as Protestants. Hundreds of people fled the country to save themselves. But nearly three hundred men, women, and children were captured and killed while Queen Mary I was in charge. The people of England couldn't believe their queen could act so cruelly. They gave her a nickname: Bloody Mary.

During this time, Queen Mary I was believed to be pregnant twice. She looked pregnant and felt pregnant. But each time, a baby was never born. Afterward, she never mentioned the pregnancies again. She died childless. Now legend says that her angry ghost haunts the mirrors of children who call to her. She wants to reach through the mirror and capture them.

FACT

Today it is believed that Queen Mary I suffered from false pregnancies. False pregnancy is when a woman believes so strongly that she is pregnant that her body starts changing as if she really was.

MARY WORTH

Some who play the Bloody Mary game chant the phrase, "I believe in Mary Worth," while holding a single candle. According to local legend, Mary Worth was a witch. She lived on a farm near Chicago, Illinois, around the time of the Civil War.

At that time, many **enslaved** people tried to escape from the South to the North on a secret network of helpful people called the Underground Railroad. Many people believe that instead of providing safety to those who were seeking freedom, Mary Worth captured them. She is said to have performed evil spells on her **victims**. She would **torture** them and eventually kill them. It wasn't long before people found out what she was doing. Legend says they put an end to her dark magic by burning her alive.

FACT

Some who call upon Bloody Mary Worth claim to see their shower curtains go up in flames . . . even though their candles were far away.

Years later, a farmer and his wife built a house right on top of the remains of Mary's barn. While farming in the field, the man found a large stone. He moved it to his front yard. Then strange things started happening. His wife got locked in the house. Plates crashed to the floor. The farmer wondered if the stone he moved was from Mary's gravesite. He tried to put the stone back but could never find the right spot.

According to the legend, the hauntings continued. Years later the house burned to the ground. Since then, no one has been able to build on that property. Anytime something is built near Mary Worth's barn, it burns to the ground.

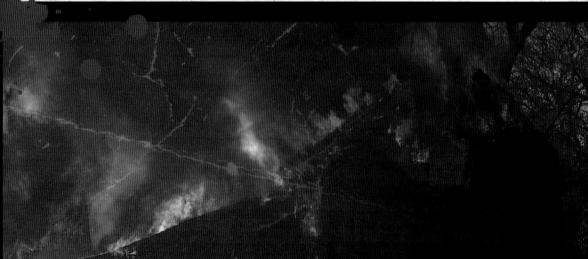

There's no historical data that proves Mary Worth existed during the time of the Civil War and the Underground Railroad. Even so, her story has become local legend in the Chicago area and continues to be told.

SKEPTIC'S NOTE

Some people say a witch named Mary Worth was killed during the Salem Witch Trials in the late 1600s. But again, there's no historical proof that Mary Worth existed at this time.

ANOTHER MARY WORTH

Others believe Mary Worth was a vain woman who was killed in a car accident. She suffered severe injuries to her face. People say she appears as an angry spirit in mirrors to **avenge** her death and bring suffering to others.

ELIZABETH BÁTHORY

Even though her name isn't Mary, Countess Elizabeth Báthory may have inspired the Bloody Mary legend. She loved looking in mirrors, and she really loved blood—the blood of young girls in particular.

Elizabeth Báthory ruled from her castle in Slovakia in the sixteenth and early seventeenth centuries. During this time, young girls in town kept disappearing. No one knew why. But Elizabeth had a plan. She was obsessed with looking young. Legend says that she believed she could look even more beautiful if she killed young women and bathed in their blood.

Elizabeth started killing castle servants. When there were no more young girls to capture in the castle, she asked the castle guards to kidnap local peasant girls and bring them to her.

SKEPTIC'S NOTE

While Elizabeth Báthory was a proven serial killer, there is no historical proof that she bathed in her victims' blood. It is simply a local legend.

SSA ELISABETHA BATHORI
S FRANCISCI DE NADASD FILII
S THOMAE DE NADASD PALATINI
CONIVX ANNO M.DL.XXXIV.

Elizabeth Báthory was born into a
powerful Hungarian family in 1560.

Elizabeth Báthory lived in the castle Hrad Cachtice. The ruins are located in what is now Slovakia.

Elizabeth continued to kill and torture girls. As the years went on, she grew careless. People soon discovered the dead bodies of young women in her castle, Hrad Cachtice. In just six years, she had tortured and killed up to 650 girls. Elizabeth became known as the Blood Countess.

Because she was a **noblewoman**, Elizabeth couldn't be put on trial or sentenced to death. Instead, a brick wall was built in front of her bedroom door to imprison her within her own castle. A few years later, she was found dead. Elizabeth Báthory now holds the Guinness World Record as the Most **Prolific** Female Murderer.

Some people who call to Elizabeth's ghost claim to find their faces instantly covered in dripping blood. When they wipe it off, hundreds of scratches mysteriously cover their face.

FACT

Elizabeth Báthory was also called Countess Dracula.

CHAPTER TWO

BLOODY MARY AROUND THE WORLD

The Bloody Mary tradition is a modern ghost story that has now traveled worldwide thanks to the internet and websites like YouTube. Now kids all over the world repeat the scary phrase in front of their mirrors. Depending on where you live in the world, the ghost's name, and how you call to her, what happens afterward can vary.

SVARTA MADAME

In Sweden, kids summon Svarta Madame, the "black woman." There are a couple different ways to call for her. Some children chant, "I don't believe in you, Svarta Madame," twelve times while standing in front of a mirror in a dark room. Others say, "Black Madame, Black Madame. Daughter of the Devil, show yourself." Then they splash water on the mirror. The woman who appears in the reflection always looks the same: glowing yellow eyes, red teeth, black skin, and green hair.

What happens next could be good or bad. You could instantly die. Or the ghost could bring you bad luck. Or possibly good fortune! This legend is so popular in Sweden that there's even been a movie made about it.

HANAKO-SAN

School bathrooms are one of the few places where adults are not watching children, so it's a great place to play a game like Bloody Mary. That may be why a ghostly figure is said to haunt school bathrooms in Japan. Japanese kids claim to hear voices, see doors slam, and watch lights flicker when they're alone in a bathroom.

Daring souls try to summon the ghost in person. They stand close to the door of the third bathroom stall and knock three times while asking, "Are you there, Hanako-san?" People have claimed to see a hand burst through the door. Legend says that the unfamiliar hand will grab the person and kill them. Others say the ghost answers, "Yes, I'm here," or the door will open a bit by itself. Inside the stall, a girlish ghost wearing an old-fashioned red dress is believed to appear.

FLUSH!

Despite the differences, the Bloody Mary tale always has ties to bathrooms, probably because they are small, dark, and have a mirror. You can easily shut off the lights, close the door, and have a little privacy while you play the Bloody Mary game. Some U.S. versions of the Bloody Mary tale go so far as to flush the toilet as part of the ritual. Sometimes the flush is needed to summon the ghost. Other times a push of the lever turns the water in the toilet red.

The ghost girl is named Toire no Hanako-san, which means, "Hanako of the Toilet." Some believe she's the spirit of a young girl who died during World War II. Local legend says that while she was playing hide-and-seek in the bathroom stall, a plane bombed the school. The building collapsed on top of her. Others believe she was a victim of bullying who hid in the third stall and was later found dead. Maybe that's why her ghost is believed to protect kids who are getting bullied.

VERONICA

In Spain and Mexico, kids tell a similar Bloody Mary story called Nueve Veces Veronica, or Nine Times Veronica. She's believed to be the spirit of a young girl who died while trying to call upon ghosts using a Bible, a red ribbon, and scissors. The legend says that Veronica and her friends were summoning ghosts in an abandoned house. Veronica didn't take it seriously, which made the ghosts mad. Before her friends could react, the scissors allegedly flew through the air, stabbing Veronica in the neck. She died immediately.

Those who are brave enough to call for Veronica's ghost light a candle in front of the mirror in a dark room just before midnight. Then, at exactly midnight, they repeat, "Veronica," nine times. Most importantly, they never laugh or make a joke, so as not to anger Veronica. People say that when she appears, the ghost is seen gripping the bloody scissors in her hands.

Some believe Veronica can answer questions about life or death. Others say she will stab you with her scissors. Still others think that nothing will happen right away, but days later your mirror may fog up with a message that reads, *I am Veronica*. She will quietly haunt your house forever. Believers say there's no way to ever get rid of her.

FACT

When a ghost appears in a physical, humanlike form that can be seen—as opposed to a cold burst of air or a spooky feeling or event—it's called an apparition.

CHAPTER THREE

DO YOU SEE WHAT I SEE?

Mirrors appear in legends all around the world. Historically, they have been seen as paths to another world, like in *Alice's Adventures in Wonderland* when Alice passes through the looking glass. In literature and art, mirrors are also often used as a way of communicating with spirits. An example of this is in *Snow White* when the evil queen talks to a ghostly face in the mirror. So it's no surprise that the Bloody Mary legend has spread far and wide, despite the mysteries surrounding it.

FACT

When using a mirror to summon a ghost, it's called **enoptromancy**.

While there are many versions of the Bloody Mary ritual, these parts remain the same: a mirror, a darkened room, and a phrase that's chanted a certain number of times. And, of course, a frightening female figure. But no one knows who this woman is or why she appears. There's no agreement on exactly what she looks like or what she will do once you're standing face-to-face with her. And that might be exactly why kids want to meet her. Many brush off the Bloody Mary legend as a simple "fear test" that lets someone try something scary in a safe place. Or is it really true?

Some people get a thrill out of summoning spirits. The expectation that something will happen is sometimes enough to make us think we saw something. That could be why the legend of Bloody Mary is still passed around to kids all over the world today. As we hear the story over and over again, we begin to believe it. But are you brave enough to say it? *Bloody Mary . . . Bloody Mary . . . Bloody Mary . . .*

SKEPTIC'S NOTE

After squinting in the darkness for a few minutes, your eyes can easily play tricks on your mind. When playing Bloody Mary, staring at your own reflection while reciting her name could be enough to trick your eyes and mind that you've seen a ghost. It could be a **hallucination**—when you think you see or hear something even if it's not there—or it could be a simple optical **illusion**.

Try staring at your own reflection in the mirror. In less than a minute, you'll see your face start changing shape. Keep staring and it will become distorted and scary looking. It might even look like an angry spirit! It turns out that if you stare at something long enough, your brain will fade out the details around it. They'll begin to blend into the background. It's called the Troxler Effect.

Stare at the red dot for twenty seconds and see what happens. More than likely, the blue circle surrounding it will start to gradually fade into the background and eventually disappear. This is just one example of this optical illusion in action.

PERRON FAMILY HAUNTING

THE GHOST STORY THAT INSPIRED HORROR MOVIES

BY EBONY JOY WILKINS

TABLE OF CONTENTS

HORROR IN HARRISVILLE

During the winter of 1970, Roger and Carolyn Perron wanted to find a home with more space for their five daughters, Andrea, Nancy, Christine, Cindy, and April. A farmhouse in rural Harrisville, Rhode Island, seemed to be the answer.

The 200-acre property was known as the Old Arnold Estate. The farmhouse had 14 rooms, a spacious porch, and plenty of room outdoors for the girls to play. But the family quickly realized that something wasn't right about their dream home. According to the family, they soon began to experience **paranormal** activity. Their story would eventually inspire the popular horror movie, *The Conjuring*.

To this day, people debate whether or not the hauntings at the Perron family home were real. Many people believe the family's accounts of paranormal activity. But skeptics believe that the family made up or exaggerated their stories in an attempt to make money and get attention from the media. Turn the page and decide for yourself. . . .

FROM THE DIRECTOR OF **SAW** AND **INSIDIOUS**

The Conjuring was released in theaters on July 19, 2013.

THE CONJURING

BASED ON THE TRUE CASE FILES OF THE WARRENS

NEW LINE CINEMA PRESENTS A SAFRAN COMPANY/EVERGREEN MEDIA GROUP PRODUCTION A JAMES WAN FILM "THE CONJURING" VERA FARMIGA PATRICK WILSON RON LIVINGSTON AND LILI TAYLOR MUSIC BY JOSEPH BISHARA EDITED BY KIRK MORRI PRODUCTION DESIGNER JULIE BERGHOFF DIRECTOR OF PHOTOGRAPHY JOHN R. LEONETTI, ASC EXECUTIVE PRODUCERS WALTER HAMADA DAVE NEUSTADTER WRITTEN BY CHAD HAYES & CAREY W. HAYES PRODUCED BY TONY DeROSA-GRUND PETER SAFRAN ROB COWAN DIRECTED BY JAMES WAN

NEW LINE CINEMA

COMING SOON

www.theconjuringmovie.co.uk

69

CHAPTER ONE

THE HAUNTING BEGINS

It didn't take long for the Perrons to determine they were not alone in their new home. When they moved in, the previous owner had a warning for them: "For the sake of your family, leave the lights on at night." But the Perrons didn't understand the warning at first. They unpacked their belongings, arranged the furniture, and explored their surroundings. As they did, strange noises, smells, and events allegedly began to occur.

MOVING TOYS

Cindy and the other Perron girls began to notice their toys were often left out of place. Cindy would set up whole villages of small toy figures. She would leave the room and soon come back to find the toys missing or rearranged. Sometimes the girls' toys would end up in the barn or in other areas around the Perrons' property. The sisters argued with one another about the missing and moved toys. But every time, the other girls would deny that they'd moved anything.

These strange events sometimes occurred when Cindy was alone in the house. She believed that someone besides her sisters must have moved her toys. Since she couldn't get rid of whoever was moving her toys, Cindy began to share them with the ghosts.

Carolyn Perron and her daughters on the steps of the family's Harrisville farmhouse

SURROUNDED BY SPIRITS

More unexplained phenomena soon began to occur.
Doors allegedly slammed closed or proved impossible
to open. Carolyn's broom went missing. It showed up in
strange places without explanation. The Perron family
often heard the sound of a broom sweeping. They found
piles of dirt that appeared to have been swept up. But no
one in the family claimed to have done the chore.

The family said that their clocks would stop at exactly
5:15 a.m. each morning. They said they often smelled
something like rotten flesh wafting through their home.

OLD ARNOLD ESTATE

The Old Arnold Estate had been the home of eight different generations of the Arnold family. Some neighbors said that many of the residents had lived and died in the home, and their spirits had stayed behind. Carolyn would eventually research the history of the home and confirm that there had been many deaths on the property. The family believed this was the cause of the haunting they experienced.

SKEPTIC'S NOTE

The Old Arnold Estate was built in 1736. The noises heard in and around the house could be explained by the old structure of the home.

At night, the family heard strange noises. They claimed to hear voices coming from the walls. According to the family, they also spotted several ghosts. One was a little boy who wandered through the house. There was also a little girl who played with the daughters' toys. Sometimes they saw a woman wearing a gray dress, her neck bent at an odd angle, as though her neck was broken.

The events were strange, but not strange enough to trouble the Perrons too much. The spirits didn't seem angry. In fact, they seemed almost kind at times.

During the first two months of their stay at the house, Cindy reported that a ghost would tuck her into bed and kiss her goodnight. She said she knew it wasn't her mother, because the ghost smelled differently. But this loving behavior would soon change into something much more sinister.

FACT

During the 1970s, the United States economy experienced a **recession**. The Perron family said that money troubles were the main reason they could not leave their rural Rhode Island farmhouse.

CHAPTER TWO

LIVING WITH THE DEAD

According to the Perron family, the atmosphere of the home soon shifted. The ghosts seemed to be less kind and welcoming than before. The Perrons felt like they were constantly being watched.

Few people believed the Perrons, however. Even Roger had a hard time believing that there were spirits in the house. But the spirits were determined to make their presence known.

HIDE-AND-SEEK

It was a hot day in August, about six months after the family moved in. The girls decided to play their favorite game— hide-and-seek. The sprawling farmhouse and surrounding property were perfect for it. Cindy found a hiding spot in the woodshed. She climbed into a large wooden box and pulled the lid closed. She held a hand over her mouth to keep from giggling.

After waiting for a while, Cindy figured her sisters were not going to find her. She tried to push at the top of the box to get out. It didn't budge. The dark, tiny space began to overwhelm Cindy. She started to panic. Cindy pushed harder and began to pound at the lid. Later, she said it felt like someone was sitting on top of it—like someone was holding the lid closed. It was getting very hot inside. She began to feel like she was running out of air.

Cindy screamed for help, but no one responded. Finally, after twenty minutes, Nancy found her and pulled open the box. According to the girls, they found no latches or locks on the box. The girls never discovered what it was that kept Cindy from escaping. They believed this was just one example of paranormal activity occurring in their new home.

EVIL SPIRITS

The paranormal activity began to get fiercer. Furniture allegedly **levitated** off the ground. The family said it sometimes slid straight across rooms. The girls' beds shook violently as they slept.

According to the daughters, one spirit pulled at the girls' limbs and hair while they slept. Another spirit allegedly lifted their beds and moved them around the bedroom. Yet another ghost is said to have hid in the corner of the girls' rooms. He stared at them with a terrifying grin as they played and slept.

Levitating furniture is often said to be a sign of the presence of spirits. However, skeptics believe that this phenomenon could be explained by people hallucinating, or imagining things that aren't there. The Perrons only have their own claims to back up these experiences. There is no proof that their furniture levitated.

Cindy claimed that one of the ghosts whispered into her ears at night. The spirit told her that seven dead soldiers were hidden in the walls of the house. She began to have awful nightmares.

Whenever the girls would yell for help, their parents couldn't hear them. According to Andrea, the house would somehow muffle their screams and cries.

As the spirits became physically aggressive, Roger and Carolyn knew they needed help. The family started to become scared for their safety. They now understood the previous owner's warning, ". . . leave the lights on at night." But even a well-lit home didn't seem to stop their difficult guests.

THE WOMAN IN THE GRAY DRESS

The ghostly woman wearing a gray dress is said to have made Carolyn her main target. One morning she showed up in Carolyn's bedroom. She told Carolyn, "Get out. Get out. I'll drive you out with death and gloom."

Carolyn claimed to often feel the presence of a spirit nearby. She began to feel pinches on her skin. Over time, the attacks became more dangerous. Carolyn said that the ghost would find her when she was alone. She threw items at Carolyn until dark bruises and red marks appeared on her skin. It was clear to the family that the ghost didn't want the Perron family **matriarch** around much longer.

CHAPTER THREE

BATHSHEBA

The Perron family believes that the ghost in the gray dress became angry when it was clear that they weren't going to flee the home. The ghost's actions were harsher and happened more and more frequently. She continued to haunt her favorite target in the Perron family—Carolyn.

THE HAUNTINGS WORSEN

The ghost apparently found Carolyn resting on the couch one evening. Carolyn felt a pain in her leg. She could also feel blood. She moved the blanket from her lap. The blood was coming from a single puncture wound on the side of her leg. Sometime during her nap, Carolyn believed she had been stabbed with something. The wound appeared to be the exact shape and size of a knitting needle. The family believed this was a sign that the ghost wanted Carolyn gone.

FACT

The oldest daughter, Andrea Perron, has written three books about her family's experiences living with spirits. The books are titled *House of Darkness House of Light,* volumes 1–3.

HELP ARRIVES

Word traveled about the reported hauntings at the Perron home. Lorraine and Ed Warren, a husband-and-wife team who were paranormal investigators, heard about the hauntings at the Old Arnold Estate. Lorraine and Ed Warren had founded the New England Society for **Psychic** Research. Ed studied demons, while Lorraine claimed to be able to communicate with demons and other evil spirits. The Warrens went to the Perron home to help the young family figure out what was going on.

Carolyn was relieved to have help. Many hadn't believed her claims of haunting, but the Warrens did. According to Andrea, when Lorraine walked into the Perron house she immediately told them, "I feel a dark presence, and her name is Bathsheba."

The Warrens agreed with Carolyn that the house was haunted by evil spirits. They believed Bathsheba was a witch. Legend says she murdered her child and then took her own life. The Warrens also believed there had been many other terrible events that had occurred on the Perron property, including unexplained accidents and deaths.

Over the course of their careers, Lorraine and Ed Warren claimed they took on more than 10,000 paranormal investigations.

SKEPTIC'S NOTE

Many don't agree with the legend of Bathsheba. Historical records show that a woman by the name of Bathsheba Thayer Sherman lived on the property in the 1800s. While she was originally charged in an infant's death, the charges were eventually dropped. Skeptics point to historical records that suggest Bathsheba was a respectable wife and mother. She cared for her children and the children of her neighbors. They believe the baby in her care could have simply died of natural causes or an accident.

Desperate to help the young family, the Warrens attempted to cleanse the home. They organized a **séance** to try to communicate with Bathsheba. Cindy and Andrea hid nearby to watch. The girls claimed to see their mother speak in a language they had never heard. They also said that Bathsheba lifted their mother in a chair and flung Carolyn's body across the room. The girls were terrified. They believed their mother had been possessed by Bathsheba.

In this image from 1986, Richard Busch from the Committee for Scientific Investigation of Claims of the Paranormal confronts Ed and Lorraine Warren.

FACT

The Warrens were criticized by many over the course of their careers. In 1997, the New England Skeptical Society (NESS) investigated the husband-and-wife team. They gave an interview on their findings in the *Connecticut Post*. NESS claimed that the Warrens produced little, if any, scientific proof of the hauntings they investigated.

THE AMITYVILLE HAUNTING

The Warrens were also famous for investigating the Amityville Haunting. This haunting was the basis for the book *The Amityville Horror*, by Jay Anson. Several films were also made based on the events in Amityville. Today people remain divided over whether or not the haunting was a **hoax**.

The haunting began in 1975. George and Kathy Lutz moved into a home at 112 Ocean Avenue on Long Island in New York. The home had been the scene of several murders just over a year before. Soon after the Lutz family arrived, the family claimed to notice strange sounds and smells, and experienced frightening events. They left the home less than a month after moving in.

CHAPTER FOUR

NIGHTMARE OVER?

Ultimately, the Perrons believed that the Warrens' attempts to help only made matters worse. Carolyn became weak and tired. She seemed to age quickly and was not acting like herself. The séance had been so out of control that Roger asked the Warrens to leave the home.

But even after the Warrens left, the Perrons claimed that the spirits remained. The family stayed in touch with the Warrens over the years, but they never were able to rid the family of Bathsheba's curse. The Perrons simply tried their best not to disturb Bathsheba and the other spirits until they could afford to leave Harrisville.

FACT

Roger Perron was often gone while the Perrons lived at the Old Arnold Estate. He often traveled away from home for work. He was rarely the target of any of the spirits in the house. He remained skeptical for a long time about what Carolyn and their daughters experienced.

Roger and Carolyn Perron
at the family home

The five Perron daughters in
front of the Harrisville home

AFTER THE MOVE

After ten years of living with evil spirits, the Perron family had had enough. In June 1980, they sold the property and moved to Georgia.

The farmhouse had other owners after the Perrons moved on. According to Andrea, many claimed to experience paranormal activity on the property. "The man who moved in to begin the restoration on the house when we sold it left screaming without his car, without his tools, without his clothing," Andrea said in an interview. "He never went back to the house . . . and it sat vacant for years."

Actress Joey King and Andrea Perron promote *The Conjuring* on a talk show.

With their move, the family hoped they were leaving the spirits behind. But Andrea later wrote about the spirits that apparently followed them to their new home. She claims that, to this day, the Perrons are haunted by Bathsheba's curse. "The house never left us, even though we left the house. It never left us and it never will," Andrea said.

THE CONJURING

The Conjuring is a horror movie inspired by the Perron family's experiences. The film was shot in North Carolina and directed by James Wan. Lorraine Warren gave the filmmakers advice on the project.

Similar to real life, the movie shows the Warrens helping the Perrons rid their home of the evil spirits. The Warrens bring in a team of paranormal investigators. Bathsheba is angered at their presence. She possesses Carolyn's body, just as the Perrons believe it occurred in real life. However, in the film, Bathsheba attempts to get Carolyn to hurt one of her children as she had done. There are no reports that Carolyn was tempted to hurt one of her daughters in real life.

The entire family was invited to the set during the filming of *The Conjuring*. Carolyn decided not to go at the last minute. While the daughters were giving an interview on the set, a wild wind is said to have torn through the area. Later the Perron daughters received bad news. They learned that Carolyn had fallen and broken her hip at the same time of this strange event. Andrea believes this was a sign from Bathsheba. The ghost was still haunting them—and warning them not to dig up the past.

Life with evil spirits was not what the Perrons had expected when they moved into their dream farmhouse. To this day, there is much debate over whether or not the haunting in Harrisville was a hoax. But whether these ghosts were real or imagined, the Perron family had to learn to live with them for the rest of their lives.

FACT

Vera Farmiga and Patrick Wilson played Lorraine and Ed Warren in *The Conjuring*. The actors spent several days learning from the real-life Lorraine Warren before they filmed. Farmiga and Wilson also starred in *The Conjuring* 2. The sequel is based on the Enfield Haunting in which a family in England was victim to a **poltergeist** haunting.

The real-life Perron sisters (top) pose on the set of *The Conjuring* with the actresses who played them in the movie (bottom).

SKEPTIC'S NOTE

Aside from their own claims, there is no proof that the Perron family experienced paranormal activity. A recent resident of the home, Norma Sutcliffe, believes they made it all up.

THE
BELL WITCH

AN AMERICAN GHOST STORY

BY MEGAN COOLEY PETERSON

TABLE OF CONTENTS

AFRAID OF THE DARK

The Bell family from Adams, Tennessee, feared the dark. From 1817 to 1821, a poltergeist haunted the family every night. It pulled their hair and overturned furniture. It threw back bedsheets and choked the children. The ghost, nicknamed the Bell Witch, even allegedly killed one member of the Bell family.

The Bells were, by all accounts, a normal family. John and Lucy married in 1782 and had nine children. The family attended church and school. They were friendly with their neighbors. So what made this ghost haunt them? And was there really a ghost at all? Some skeptics believe the Bells invented the ghost for attention. Other people believe the haunting actually occurred.

The Bell log cabin is the only original structure that still exists from the Bells' farm. The Bell family used it as an outbuilding.

CHAPTER ONE

THE TROUBLE BEGINS

In 1804, John and Lucy Bell and their children moved from North Carolina to Tennessee. They had heard of the area's rich farmland and dense forests. They purchased property on the Red River, which included a house and barns. John cleared some of the land and started farming. Life in Tennessee seemed perfect.

Until the trouble began.

The Bell homestead sat on the Red River. The fertile land was perfect for farming.

It was the summer of 1817. While working in the field, John stumbled upon a strange animal sitting between two rows of corn. It looked like a dog with the head of a rabbit. John raised his gun and shot at the creature, but it ran off.

The strange sightings didn't end there. A few days later, John and Lucy's son Drew spotted a large turkey perched on a fence. As Drew approached the bird, he saw that it wasn't a turkey at all. The bird flapped its large wings and took off. Drew had no idea what kind of bird it might be.

Betsy, the youngest daughter, went for a walk in the woods near the house around this same time. She saw a girl in a green dress climbing one of the oak trees. She had never seen this girl before and found it strange.

A few days later, one of the Bells' enslaved workers reported seeing a large, black dog in the road. This dog followed him every night when he went to visit his wife. She was also enslaved and lived with a different family. As soon as the man arrived at his wife's door each night, the dog ran away.

Little did the Bells know, these odd events were about to take a terrifying turn.

WITCHES
AND FAMILIARS

Is it possible that the Bells' strange animal sightings had
something to do with the paranormal? According to folklore,
witches had animals called "familiars." These animals could
assist a witch in her magical workings. A familiar could spy
on people, steal from them, and even attack them. Black cats
were said to be favored by witches. But other animals
could also serve as familiars, such as toads,
dogs, and other small animals.

CHAPTER TWO

UNSEEN HANDS

Members of the Bell family didn't think much of the strange creatures they'd seen around the farm. But then one night, strange scratching and banging sounds began outside the house. The family went outside to investigate, and the sounds stopped. Each night as the family went to bed, the scratching and banging started. And each time they went outside, the sounds were replaced with silence.

The strange sounds soon moved inside the house, starting in the boys' bedroom. A sound like rats gnawing on the bedposts woke the boys. The two eldest sons, John Jr. and Drew, got up to kill the rats. But as soon as their feet hit the floor, the gnawing stopped. They looked under the beds and found no rats or chew marks. Once the brothers climbed back into bed, the gnawing started again. The boys stayed up half the night searching for the source of the gnawing.

SKEPTIC'S NOTE

Scratching sounds can be caused by tree branches moving in the wind or animals crawling around the house.

The gnawing sounds continued for weeks, now in all the bedrooms. The Bells also heard dogs fighting and the sound of chains being dragged across the floor. Whenever someone lit a candle, the sounds ceased.

The family examined every room in the house. They moved furniture and pulled up rugs. But no one could find the source of the nightly racket. It steadily grew worse. Along with the gnawing, the Bell family heard lips smacking and the sound of someone choking. The noises stopped every night between one and three in the morning.

JOHN BELL'S ILLNESS

John Bell began to experience some strange health problems around this time. His tongue would swell up in his mouth. Sometimes he was unable to eat. John said it felt as if a small piece of wood had been lodged sideways in his mouth, pushing at his cheeks.

SKEPTIC'S NOTE

Rodents hide from bright lights and people. If the Bells had rats in their house, it's not unusual that the rats would have hidden from view.

A TERRIFYING TURN

After about a year, the strange sounds turned into poltergeist-like activity. One night, 6-year-old Richard Williams had just fallen asleep. Suddenly it felt as though someone was twisting his hair. Unseen hands pulled so hard he was lifted right out of bed. "It felt like the top of my head had been taken off," he later recalled. Something also pulled Betsy's hair. Covers were torn off beds while the family slept.

John and Lucy had no idea what was causing the paranormal activity. They began staying up all night to protect their children. They decided to invite their neighbors Dr. James Johnson and his wife to spend the night in their home. They wanted someone outside the family to witness the events.

Before bedtime, James read some passages from the Bible. He also prayed that the Bell family would no longer be haunted. Despite the prayer, the activity started up as soon as everyone went to bed. Chairs overturned, and covers flew off beds.

James tried speaking with the entity. "In the name of the Lord, what or who are you? What do you want and why are you here?" he asked. But the entity wouldn't answer. James concluded it had to be some kind of spirit. But what did it want with the Bell family?

FAMOUS POLTERGEIST

The Enfield poltergeist from England is one of the most famous poltergeist cases. In 1977, Peggy Hodgson and her daughters, Janet and Margaret, began to experience frightening incidents. The girls' bedroom in this photograph is where most of the events occurred. Furniture moved on its own. The girls flew across the room. Fires started on their own. The ghost even allegedly spoke through 11-year-old Janet. After 18 months, the activity stopped.

CHAPTER THREE

THE GHOST TARGETS BETSY BELL

The ghost soon set its sights on another family member—Betsy. Betsy's cheeks turned red from being slapped by the ghost. Sometimes Betsy couldn't breathe. It felt as if someone was choking her. She also felt as though something was sticking her with sharp pins. Her hair comb would be ripped from her head and tossed to the ground. A woman's laughter could be heard, as if it took joy in Betsy's pain. They assumed the voice belonged to the ghost.

SKEPTIC'S NOTE

Betsy's hair comb could have simply fallen out. The family was already on edge. They might have blamed normal, everyday occurrences on the ghost.

Betsy's parents were terrified the ghost might try to kill their daughter. They sent her to her friends' houses to sleep, hoping the ghost wouldn't follow. But it harassed Betsy no matter where she slept.

This drawing of Betsy Bell was first published in 1894 in *An Authenticated History of the Bell Witch* by M. V. Ingram.

A PRESIDENTIAL GHOST HUNTER?

In the summer of 1819, word of the Bell Witch reached future U.S. president Andrew Jackson. According to legend, Jackson came to the farm to investigate for himself. Within a mile of the farm, Jackson's wagon wheels locked up. Jackson blamed the event on the Bell Witch. The spirit answered that it was responsible and let the wagon continue. At the house, one of his men bragged that he could kill the witch. The witch lifted the man and tossed him about the house.

BAD MEDICINE

Betsy became desperate to rid herself of the ghost. A doctor came to the house, claiming he could cure her. He had mixed up a special medicine for her to drink. Betsy's friend Theny Thorn advised her against it, but she drank it anyway.

Within moments of taking the medicine, Betsy vomited. Theny noticed something strange about what she had thrown up. Upon closer examination, the vomit was full of pins and needles. The ghost laughed as Theny cleaned up the mess. Everyone agreed the ghost must have dropped the pins and needles into the vomit when no one was looking. No one, it seemed, could cure Betsy of her troubles.

SKEPTIC'S NOTE

Either Betsy or Theny could have
dropped the pins into the mess
when the other wasn't looking.

FACT

Theny collected some of the
pins and needles and kept
them for the rest of her life.

Some people suggested that perhaps Betsy was the cause of the strange occurrences. She may have been making the whole thing up for attention. But that theory ended when the ghost began speaking. At first it only whistled when asked a question. Then the ghost began to speak in a low whisper. "I am the spirit of a person who was buried in the woods nearby," the ghostly voice said. "The grave has been disturbed, my bones **disinterred** and scattered, and one of my teeth was lost under this house, and I am here looking for that tooth."

As the family searched the house for a lost tooth, the ghost cackled with glee. It said it was all a joke to fool John, whom the ghost called Old Jack. The Bell Witch also took an interest in Betsy's boyfriend, Joshua Gardner. The ghost would whisper at Betsy in a hushed voice not to marry Joshua. No one could figure out why the ghost disliked Joshua.

FACT

The Bell Witch haunting inspired the horror movie *The Blair Witch Project.*

SIMILARITIES TO THE SALEM WITCH TRIALS

In 1692 and 1693, 19 people were found guilty of **witchcraft** and hanged in Salem, Massachusetts. Like the Bell Witch haunting, the activity centered around young girls. They spoke in strange voices. Unseen hands pinched and bit them. Their bodies contorted. The girls mainly accused women of using witchcraft against them. One of the men accused, Giles Corey, refused to continue with his trial. He was tortured to death. After the trials, one accuser admitted to making the whole thing up.

More than 200 people were accused of witchcraft during the Salem Witch Trials.

CHAPTER FOUR

A DEADLY END

The year was 1820, and the Bell family had experienced three years of unexplained phenomena. For most of this time, John Bell suffered discomfort in his mouth. But as the years wore on, his pain grew steadily worse. The swelling in his mouth became so severe that he couldn't talk or eat for 10 or 15 hours at a time. The muscles in his face began to contort, and he was often too sick to get out of bed. Oddly, as John's symptoms grew worse, Betsy's improved.

On the morning of December 19, John did not wake up at his usual time. When the family could not wake him, John Jr. went to the medicine cabinet. Inside, he found a strange vial containing dark liquid. No one had ever seen this vial before. "It's useless for you to try to revive Old Jack," the ghost said. "I have got him this time; he will never get up from that bed again." The ghostly voice also admitted that it had fed John the medicine.

FACT

The Bell Witch allegedly adored Lucy Bell and never bothered her.

This image, showing the scene of John Bell's death, was published in M. V. Ingram's 1894 account of the Bell Witch haunting.

FACT

A bit of the strange medicine was given to a cat. Within moments of drinking the liquid, the cat supposedly died.

The doctor soon arrived at the Bell house. He had never seen the vial before either. John's breath reeked of the medicine. When the doctor tossed the vial into the fire, a bright blue haze shot up the chimney. On December 20, 1820, John Bell died. His official cause of death: poisoning.

A few months after John's death, the Bell Witch told the family it would return in seven years. As promised, the ghost allegedly returned to the Bell farm in February 1828. According to Richard Williams, the witch started up with her old behavior. She scratched the bed posts and snatched off covers.

The Bell Witch claimed she would return in 1935 to visit John Bell's closest relative, but there is no proof she ever did. After about two or three weeks, the ghost vanished.

CHAPTER FIVE

WHO WAS THE BELL WITCH?

No one knows for sure who the Bell Witch was. At the time of the haunting, many people blamed a local woman named Kate Batts. They believed she was a witch. Kate owned a farm near the Bells. She and John allegedly had a disagreement when the Bells first moved into the area, and Kate was said to have cursed John Bell.

Another theory is that the Bell Witch was a poltergeist. Some paranormal experts believe a poltergeist isn't a ghost at all. These experts say that an individual can cause a ghostlike disturbance using only their minds. This person might be going through physical or emotional stress and not realize they're causing the activity.

FACT

After Lucy Bell died, no one ever lived in the Bell house again. It was eventually torn down.

BELL WITCH

To the north was the farm of John Bell, an early, prominent settler from North Carolina. According to legend, his family was harried during the early 19th century by the famous Bell Witch. She kept the household in turmoil, assaulted Bell, and drove off Betsy Bell's suitor. Even Andrew Jackson who came to investigate, retreated to Nashville after his coach wheels stopped mysteriously. Many visitors to the house saw the furniture crash about them and heard her shriek, sing, and curse.

TENNESSEE HISTORICAL COMMISSION

This historic marker in Adams tells a brief history of the hauntings the Bell family endured.

Could someone in or close to the family have faked the haunting? Some suggest a man named Richard Powell did just that. Powell was a teacher who knew the Bell family. He wanted to marry Betsy, but she was already dating Joshua Gardner. Some say he made up the haunting to scare Joshua away. Betsy did eventually marry Powell.

More than 200 years after the haunting began, the story of the Bell Witch continues to captivate audiences. We'll never know for sure who—or what—caused the ghostlike activity that haunted the Bell family. But it can be fun to guess.

A FAKED MANUSCRIPT?

Richard Williams Bell allegedly wrote about his experiences with the witch almost 30 years after they happened. His account was included in *An Authenticated History of the Famous Bell Witch* by M.V. Ingram. But Richard Williams's original manuscript has never been found. Some believe Ingram made it up.

FACT

The Bell Witch Cave near the Bell farm site
is open to the public. The witch's face is
allegedly etched into stone inside the cave.

GLOSSARY

afterworld (AF-tur-wurld)—a place where beings go after they die

allegedly (uh-LEDGE-id-lee)—said to be true or to have happened, but without proof

apparition (ap-uh-RISH-uhn)—the visible appearance of a ghost

avenge (uh-VENJ)—to punish someone who has harmed you

Aztec (AZ-tek)—a member of an indigenous people who lived in Mexico before Spanish people settled there

convent (KAHN-vent)—a building where a group of women who have devoted their lives to the church live

disinterred (dis-in-TERD)—dug up something that was buried

enoptromancy (en-OP-troh-mehn-see)—using a mirror to summon a ghost

enslaved (in-SLAYVED)—a person who is enslaved is forced to be the legal property of another person and to obey him or her

evidence (EV-i-duhns)—information and facts that help prove something is or is not true

familiar (fuh-MIL-yur)—an animal believed to be under the control of a witch or other magical being

folklore (FOHK-lor)—tales and customs among a group of people

hallucination (huh-loo-sih-NAY-shuhn)—an experience of seeing or hearing things that are not real

hoax (HOHKS)—a trick that makes people believe something that is not true

illusion (ih-LOO-zhuhn)—a deceiving or misleading image

levitate (LEV-i-tate)—to hover in the air

matriarch (MAY-tree-ark)—a woman who is the head of a family

mythology (mith-AWL-uh-jee)—a group of old or ancient stories told again and again that help connect people with their past

noblewoman (NOH-buhl-wum-uhn)—a woman of a high social class

paranormal (pair-uh-NOR-muhl)—having to do with an event that has no scientific explanation

persecution (pur-suh-KYOO-shuhn)—the act of continually treating someone cruely and unfairly

poltergeist (POHL-tur-guyst)—a ghost that causes physical events, such as objects moving

prolific (proh-LIF-ik)—producing a large amount of something

psychic (SYE-kik)—relating to events that are not able to be explained by natural laws

recession (ri-SESH-uhn)—a time when business slows down and more workers than usual are unemployed

remorse (ri-MORS)—a strong feeling of guilt or regret

ritual (RICH-oo-uhl)—a series of actions performed in a ceremonial order

séance (SAY-ahnss)—a meeting in which one attempts to communicate with the spirits of the dead

siren (SYE-ruhn)—half-bird, half-woman creature that lures sailors to their deaths by singing

skeptic (SKEP-tik)—someone who doubts or questions beliefs

summon (SUHM-uhn)—to call upon or send for

torture (TOR-chur)—to cause someone extreme pain or suffering

victim (VIK-tuhm)—a person who is hurt, killed, or made to suffer

witchcraft (WICH-kraft)—the practice of magic

INDEX